T0195919

IT
IS A
MERCY
DIFFERENCE

CASTER MTWALE

WESTBOW
PRESS®
A DIVISION OF THOMAS NELSON
& ZONDERVAN

WestBow Press books may be ordered through booksellers or by contacting:

WestBow Press
A Division of Thomas Nelson & Zondervan
1663 Liberty Drive
Bloomington, IN 47403
www.westbowpress.com
844-714-3454

Scripture taken from the New King James Version®. Copyright © 1982 by Thomas Nelson. Used by permission. All rights reserved.

ISBN: 979-8-3850-1682-2 (sc)
ISBN: 979-8-3850-1683-9 (e)

Library of Congress Control Number: 2024900732

Print information available on the last page.

WestBow Press rev. date: 01/18/2024

This book is dedicated to the Holy Spirit. Since early on in my Christian life, He has been there to lead, teach, and guide me. He has been my helper all my life. Thank you, Holy Spirit, and to God be the glory.

Blessed be the Lord God of our fathers, who has put such a thing as this is the king's heart, to beautify the house of the Lord which is in Jerusalem, and has extended mercy to me before the king and his counselors, and before all the king's mighty princes. So, I was encouraged, as the hand of the Lord my God was upon me; and I gathered leading men of Israel to go up with me. (Ezra 7:27-28)

CONTENTS

Introduction... xi

1   What is Mercy?.. 1

2   Why Do We Need Mercy?.. 6

3   The Importance of Asking God for Mercy 15

4   Let Mercy Stand Alone 20

5   Be Willing to Let Go of Your Little Things............. 27

6   Trust in God's Mercy, Not Your Abilities................ 40

7   Who Qualifies for Mercy?...................................... 46

8   Ask for Mercy That Your Spiritual Eyes Might
    Be Opened...55

9   Have Mercy on Others So You Can Receive
    Mercy for Yourself... 62

10 What Shall We Do Then? 73

About the Author..81

CONTENTS

INTRODUCTION

Seasons come and seasons go; however, the search for what could make life a little easier never goes away. The quest to simplify life is ingrained in the very nature of our human DNA. It is one of the very forces that has led to many inventions of our time. It is also the very force that has inspired many technological discoveries. These inventions and technologies are widely known and used today. All kinds of resources have been poured out to make these inventions and discoveries possible, including but not limited to funding, time, energy, and learning.

Wouldn't it be a life changing to know that there is one invention that you have never used or have used a very little? The invention I speak of is the mercy of God. God himself is the inventor of mercy. He invented mercy to help His creation—you and me. He invented mercy to make our lives not just a little easier but a lot better. Unlike the inventions and technologies that, in most cases if not all cases, require some form of money, time, energy, connections, and learning, the mercy of God requires only faith—the faith that God will give to you what you ask of Him. He will show you mercy whether you have money, religion, energy, education, connections, or title. He will have compassion on you.

As we shall see in this book, the inventor of

mercy—God—wants you to come as you are. Consider this to be His personal invitation for you to discover for yourself that, regardless of who you are, where you have been, what you have done, or where you have come from, He still wants to show you His loving kindness. He wants to have mercy on you. His mercy is unfailing.

CHAPTER 1

WHAT IS MERCY?

> How excellent [is] thy lovingkindness, O
> God! therefore the children of men put
> their trust under the shadow of thy wings.
> (Psalm36:7)

It was yet another moment in which I was enduring severe back pain from an injury I had sustained during my previous job five years back. I had seen a chiropractor and gone through a proposed treatment. The treatment ended, but my back pain didn't. It only got worse as time went on. I had also prayed that God would grant me healing, but I didn't receive an answer. Nights were hard for me. No sleeping position would to relieve me from pain.

On this day when the severe back pain started, I felt

as if my back was on fire, so I sat on a chair. Unlike other times, on this particular night I cried out to God, "God, have mercy on me and heal my back!" Suddenly I felt as if someone took an ice pack and put it on the back of my neck. From there, the feeling trickled down, and every inch where the droplets from the ice pack touched as it passed through, the pain was wiped out. That process took a few seconds. To my big surprise, when it was finished, I was left with a back that was absolutely free from pain. I felt so much lighter. Instinctively, I stood up—and there was no pain. I bent down a few times. Prior to this, bending had caused me an excruciating amount of pain, but there was no pain. That was when I realized that I had been miraculously healed!

I must admit I did not believe that this was actually true. After all, two doctors at different locations had used X-rays to confirm that I had a terrible back injury. Nevertheless, my thinking could not change my experience of God's mercy. It was about eight o'clock at night, and since I had not been able to sleep for days, I went to bed. I woke up at eight the next morning, still pain free.

A few days later, I had an opportunity to have additional X-rays done of my back. The doctor reported, "This is one of the healthiest backs I have ever seen. You have a very good back." To this day, I have never had any back problems. I am totally healed. What did I do to become healed? I asked God to have mercy on me. And He did! Would you ask Him, too, for mercy right now? Tell Him what troubles you, for He is the Father of mercies and all comfort. "Blessed *be* the God and Father of our Lord Jesus Christ, the Father of mercies and God of all comfort" (2 Corinthians 1:3). Tell Him, "God have mercy on me."

I have now experienced seventeen years of freedom from back pain. My cry for mercy from God made we well.

For many of us, the word *mercy* has been used so many times it appears to have little value, meaning, or power. This is why it is so important to highlight what mercy is and why it is so important to receive and give it. This is because, in this life, you are going to come to the point (if you are not there yet) where only mercy can ease your misery, land you that business opportunity, save or restore your marriage, heal you, help you purchase your dream home, or get you out of trouble. Life will bring situations, demands, or circumstances to the place where nothing else will rescue you but mercy.

Mercy, for many, is simply known as the withholding of punishment. But from the biblical standpoint, mercy means something much deeper. Mercy is the loving kindness of God. "Show Your marvelous lovingkindness by Your right hand, O You who save those who trust *in You* From those who rise up *against them*." (Psalm 17:7). The Hebrew word *checed* here is translated as "lovingkindness." in the King James Version. In the Old Testament, the Hebrew word <u>*checed*</u> in the authorized version (King James Version) is found 248 times: 149 times it is translated as "mercy," 40 times it is translated as "kindness," and 30 times it is translated as "loving-kindness" (or "lovingkindness").

> *How* excellent [is] thy lovingkindness, O God! therefore the children of men put their trust under the shadow of thy wings. (Psalm 36:7)

In addition, two Greek words, *eleeo* and *aleos*, are translated in the authorized version as "mercy" in the New Testament. They are used fifty-nine times. Mathew 5:7: "Blessed are the merciful: for they shall receive mercy" (KJV). From this we learn that mercy is not simply the withholding of judgment and punishment; rather, it is the act of giving gracious help or having compassion for someone who is afflicted. In short, mercy is receiving something we want even though we have not earned, deserved, or merited it. Instead, it is what we have been given to benefit or profit us. This is why the Bible says, "But God shows his love for us in that while we were still sinners, Christ died for us" (Romans 5:8). That was God's demonstration of mercy. Mercy is kindness and compassion.

The Bible records several incidents of people crying out to Jesus for mercy during His earthly ministry. In one incident, a father brought his epileptic son to Jesus's disciples hoping they would cure him from the disease, but they couldn't. When he saw Jesus, he cried out for mercy, and Jesus responded and rebuked the demon, which came out of the child. Matthew 17:14–18 records the father's plea for his son's healing this way:

> And when they had come to the multitude, a man came to Him, kneeling down to Him and saying, *"Lord, have mercy on my son*, for he is an epileptic and suffers severely; for he often falls into the fire and often into the water. So I brought him to Your disciples, but they could not cure him." Then Jesus answered and said, "O faithless

and perverse generation, how long shall I be
with you? How long shall I bear with you?
Bring him here to Me." And Jesus rebuked
the demon, and it came out of him; and the
child was cured from that very hour.

God always responds to cries of mercy. This is because
the cry of mercy puts God in a position to act on us and on
our behalf according to His goodness and kindness and not
according to our deeds. When we cry out for mercy from
Him, we are basically telling Him that we don't deserve
what we are asking for. We are asking God to bypass our
shortcomings and imperfections. In a sense, it is our way of
humbling ourselves before Him. The Bible says that grace
(unmerited favor) follows humility: "But He gives more
grace. Therefore He says: "God resists the proud, But gives
grace to the humble" (James 4:6–7).

CHAPTER 2

WHY DO WE NEED MERCY?

The Lord is merciful and gracious, Slow to anger, and abounding in mercy. He will not always strive with us, Nor will He keep His anger forever. He has not dealt with us according to our sins, Nor punished us according to our iniquities. For as the heavens are high above the earth, So great is His mercy toward those who fear Him; As far as the east is from the west, So far has He removed our transgressions from us. As a father pities his children, So the Lord pities those who fear Him. For He knows our frame; He remembers that we are dust. (Psalm 103:8–14)

I had just gotten to the front porch of one of the properties I was managing. I was there to check on the property. The tenants had been living there for a little while and had not been paying attention to a leaking toilet and had apparently left it running continuously day and night. I didn't know it, but the city officials had taken note of the increased water usage, and they had scheduled to shut the water off that same day. The day before I had also asked the handyman to tend to anything that needed fixing, and that is when he found out about the leaking toilet, which he fixed.

When the city worker got there, he headed directly to the water meter. I followed him there. I asked him what he was up to. He told me he was going to shut off the water. I asked him why, and he said his department had seen from the main meter that the dial had been going nonstop, and that meant there was leak. They were going to cut off the water until the leak was fixed. I informed him that I had no idea that it had been happening for quite some time, but just the day before I had asked my handyman to fix the problem. The city worker told me that, since that was the case, he was going to test it again before he shut off the water. He retested the system and found no water leakage.

He took extra time to explain to me that it is very important for me, as a property manager, to stay on top of things to avoid costly lawsuits that might be caused by negligent tenants. He further explained that he had been in court so many times with cases like this where tenants didn't report a serious problem on time, and then the tenants had to take the landlord to court to demand monetary compensation. He said, "The saddest part is that they always win with this kind of stuff." That was an eye-opener for me.

I was very new to all this. And, as a property manager, it was crucial that I gain this priceless knowledge. God was merciful to me that day by allowing me to go there at the same time that city worker was going there. The tenants had no reason to drag me to court. Their actions had triggered a possible loss of water service as well as extra fees for turning the water back on. This knowledge has helped me to stay on top of things. I no longer allow any loopholes unfaithful tenants could use to take advantage of me. This was a kind of mercy that I didn't even know how to ask for—the kind of mercy that makes sure you don't fall into traps that have been laid out for you. This is the kind of mercy that not only protects you but also teaches you how to avoid traps.

We need mercy because, by nature, we are a fallen people. According to God's standards, we deserve nothing good; rather, we deserve judgment and punishment. To the contrary, we tend to think that mercy is not that important in our lives in this day and age because, for the most part, we believe we deserve all that we have—our houses, our cars, our well-behaved children, our jobs, our spouses. The list goes on and on. As a matter of fact, we have worked very hard to have all that we have. We fail to realize that, if it was not for God's mercy, we would not have all these things that we have to show to ourselves and others. We forget that even our ability to wake up every morning and go wherever we have to go is due to His mercies, which are new every morning. "Through the Lord's mercies we are not consumed, Because His compassions fail not. They are new every morning; Great *is* Your faithfulness" (Lamentation 3:22–23).

We also need mercy because our abilities, talents, wealth,

fame, titles, education, and experience alone are not enough to bring about the abundant life that will give us satisfaction in all areas of our lives whether it be physically, mentally, emotionally, or psychologically. The mercy of God, which is His kindness and compassion, is what makes the distinction between one person and another, success and failure. I will later speak more of how the mercy of God can make a distinction between us and others for our good.

God, in His loving kindness, shows mercy to all even without being asked. This explains why you and I are still breathing. This is a kind of mercy of God that we get daily even without asking or acknowledging it. It is the kind of mercy that causes us to be at the right place at the right time to meet the right people.

However, there is a kind of mercy that we will not have unless we acknowledge that we need mercy and ask for it. "Ask, and it will be given to you; seek, and you will find; knock, and it will be opened to you" (Matthew 7:7). Thinking that we deserve all that we will pray for is very foolish. God is not obligated to give us anything for He has already given us His only begotten Son who died for us: "For God so loved the world that He gave His only begotten Son, that whoever believes in Him should not perish but have everlasting life " (John 3:16). In Him we have all that we need. However, because of our shortcomings, He continues to pour out His mercy every single moment of our lives.

I was in great distress and desperate to get out of a situation that I was in. I prayed for God's intervention, and I clearly sensed that I was supposed to wait—help would come. Instead of waiting as I had been instructed by the Holy Spirit, I decided to ignore that instruction, and I took matters into my own hands. I took all of my life's savings and borrowed more on top of that and poured it into something that I thought should have been done at that time. I was not prepared for what happened next. The person who was supposed to deliver the service I had paid for ran away with my money and refused to have anything to do with me. I asked several friends to help me, and they all refused. I was left with no money, no friends, and nowhere to go. I wept as asked God to forgive me and help me and have mercy on me. Unexpectedly, shortly after my pleas, a person whom I had never met came to me and asked me what I needed. I explained my problem to her, and she told husband. Together, they solved my problem in days, and I didn't have to pay a single penny. I looked back at my disobedience to that instruction of "wait," and then I looked back to the faithfulness, loving kindness, and mercy of God, and I was filled with gratitude for who God is. God chose not to deal with me for my disobedience to the instructions that He had previously given me; instead, he showed me His mercy. He is very merciful.

This explains why, in the Old Testament, when God ordered Moses to build the Ark of the Covenant, He specifically instructed Moses to make a mercy seat to cover the contents of the ark. Why cover the contents of the ark? This was to protect the contents, one of which was the Ten Commandments or God's law, which is the Word of God. The Ten Commandments were the instructions that God gave His people so they would know how to conduct themselves, how to treat each other, and how to relate to Him. The mercy seat was where God met with humanity, "And there I will meet with you, and I will speak with you from above the mercy seat" (Exodus 25:22). If God had chosen to meet His people according to His word, according to the instructions that He had previously given them, they would all have been consumed. But instead, He chose to meet them according to His mercy. The mercy seat is an example of how God has put our sin under His mercy seat and covered it by the blood of Jesus. If it were not for the mercy seat, you and I could not come into the presence of God because God would have to judge us for every sin we commit. We all stand guilty before God. The mercy seat is what gives us a privilege to stand before Him and ask for help regardless of what we have done. When you come to God on the ground of mercy, you are assured to have the answer for your petition. It becomes all about Him and His perfection. He sees you from the lens of mercy and not from the lens of your failed marriage, bad business deals, addictions, bad choices, anger issues, lack of education, or patterns of unfaithfulness.

God is perfect, and in order for us to match His perfection, we must be perfect just as He is perfect. "Therefore you shall be perfect, just as your Father in heaven is perfect" (Matthew 5:48). And when we fall short of His perfection (which we do), we deserve nothing but judgment and punishment. Nevertheless, God does not deal with us based on our imperfections; rather, he deals with us based on His mercy. This is why the Bible says that mercy triumphs over judgment (James 2:13).

ACKNOWLEDGE THE
PRESENCE OF MERCY

In order for us to continue to have and enjoy healed bodies, answered prayers, functional families, outstanding performances, good health, and whatever valuables that comes to mind, we must continue to acknowledge and ask for God's mercy. This does not mean that we have not done our part to obtain all these things. Instead, it simply says that there is One who sits in heaven who initiated and blessed us with all these things. Even though there are others who seem to qualify more than we do, we seem to fare well compared to them. This reminds me of a former friend of mine who got a very good, high-paying job in one of the Fortune 500 companies even though she did not have any experience in what she was hired for. There were others who had more qualifications than she had. However, she was hired and was trained to do the job. She later told me that, when she was applying for that job, she did not pay attention to what she did *not* have. Instead, she paid attention to what God could do for her. She acknowledged that she did not deserve to have the job. Even though she had the required education, she lacked the experience. The mercy of God bypassed her lack of experience and granted her the job.

WHAT WE HAVE CAN
BE TAKEN AWAY

We must know and acknowledge that whatever we have today, we have it because of His mercy. And if He decides to allow those things to be taken away from us, He can in a matter of days if not hours. (Note that the word *allow* shows that God does not personally take away what He has given us. However, He can allow—as he did in Job's case—for circumstances to take things away from us). It happened to Job; in one day he lost everything. The Bible explains Job's loss this way:

> Now there was a day when his sons and daughters were eating and drinking wine in their oldest brother's house; and a messenger came to Job and said, "The oxen were plowing and the donkeys feeding beside them, when the Sabeans raided them and took them away—indeed they have killed the servants with the edge of the sword; and I alone have escaped to tell you!" While he was still speaking, another also came and said, "The fire of God fell from heaven and burned up the sheep and the servants, and consumed them; and I alone have escaped to tell you!" While he was still speaking, another also came and said, "The Chaldeans formed three bands, raided the camels and took them away, yes, and killed the servants with the edge of the sword; and I alone have escaped to tell you!" While he was still speaking, another also came and said, "Your sons and daughters were eating and drinking wine in their oldest brother's house, and suddenly a great wind came from across the wilderness

and struck the four corners of the house, and it fell on the young people, and they are dead; and I alone have escaped to tell you!" Then Job arose, tore his robe, and shaved his head; and he fell to the ground and worshiped. And he said: " Naked I came from my mother's womb, And naked shall I return there. The Lord gave, and the Lord has taken away; Blessed be the name of the Lord. (Job 1:13–21)

After all this happened, Job said, "He gives and takes away." Keep in mind that Job did not do anything to cause these losses in his life. Everything was taken from him simply because the enemy wanted it that way. It is not always what we do, what we say, affirmations we speak, what we eat, or how much we give that determines or guarantee us great health, protection, or success in life. Though it is good and important to make good decisions in these areas of our lives, they are not everything. It is all because of God's goodness, loving-kindness—God's mercy. The mercy of God completes things. The mercy of God grants us what we have not earned.

This is why it is important to know that, after we have done all that we know to do naturally or spiritually, we must humble ourselves and acknowledge and appreciate the presence of God and His mercy in our lives. Also, we must acknowledge our desperate need for mercy.

CHAPTER 3

THE IMPORTANCE OF ASKING GOD FOR MERCY

And Jesus went away from there and withdrew to the district of Tyre and Sidon. And behold, a Canaanite woman from that region came out and was crying, "Have mercy on me, O Lord, Son of David; my daughter is severely oppressed by a demon." But he did not answer her a word. And his disciples came and begged him, saying, "Send her away, for she is crying out after us." He answered, "I was sent only to the lost sheep of the house of Israel." But she came and knelt before him, saying, "Lord, help me." And he answered, "It is not right

to take the children's bread and throw it
to the dogs." She said, "Yes, Lord, yet even
the dogs eat the crumbs that fall from their
masters' table." Then Jesus answered her,
"O woman, great is your faith! Be it done
for you as you desire." And her daughter
was healed instantly. (Mathew 15:21-28)

Now that we know our need for mercy, we must also
understand the importance of asking God for mercy. As I said
earlier, God has already given us mercy and is still providing
mercy to us without being asked for it. However, in other
circumstances and situations, God will intervene with His
mercy only after He is asked for it. Even though we may pray
and fast, we still need to specifically ask for mercy when we
need it. This does not mean that prayer and fasting are not
important. I personally live a life of prayer and fasting. As
a matter of fact, a week before I got the idea of writing this
book, I had an impression in my spirit that the Lord wanted
me to fast. I spent a day praying and fasting. Three days after
that fast, it became very clear to me that God wanted me to
write a book about mercy. With this particular assignment,
God wanted me to pray and also fast so that I would gain an
understanding of what He wanted me to do. And when I did
fast and pray, the understanding came together to me without
any striving. What I am saying here is that, when we fast and
pray, we must make mention of our need for mercy.

Be anxious for nothing, but in everything by
prayer and supplication, with thanksgiving,
let your requests be made known to God;

and the peace of God, which surpasses all
understanding, will guard your hearts and
minds through Christ Jesus. (Philippians
4:6–7)

We must remember to let our request of mercy be
known to God.

The Mercy of God on a Little One

One day few years ago, my doorbell rang, and I rushed
quickly to open the door. A two-year-old blonde boy with
blue eyes (whom I will call Jelo) stood there with a social
worker. I had been expecting him as I had been told that he
needed a placement. I was a foster parent and Jelo was going
to be my foster child. I welcomed him into my home, and
he couldn't wait to start roaming around. Within minutes,
I realized that the child had severe anger issues and physical
aggression. Additionally, he couldn't speak at all. All he did
was scream. He screamed morning, afternoon, and night.
He screamed all day. It got so bad that, one day, a passerby
heard him and, thinking something horrible was happening
to the boy, called the police. When the police arrived, they
saw that the boy was okay; in fact, he was happy to see the
police and wanted the officers to hold him! It was customary
in his birth family to have police presence all the time,
so he was comfortable around them. I came to learn that
he was born addicted to methamphetamine (meth). Jelo,
among other things, was a head banger. When he was irate,

he would bang his head on the walls, the concrete floor, the bed frames, and other hard surfaces. He also couldn't comprehend what was being said to him, which made communication difficult. When I took him to the doctor, I was told that he demonstrated symptoms of autism. The evaluation for autism was scheduled but there was a long wait. Life with him was very difficult. He and I were both suffering. I was exhausted and couldn't sleep much because he was awake and screaming day and night. Even though he was in all sorts of therapies (speech, occupational, physical and behavioral), there was no improvements.

In my exhaustion, I turned to Jesus. I asked Him to have mercy on this troubled child. I asked Him to override the effects of meth addiction, calm his senses, and restructure his mind so he could understand what was said to him. I also asked that he be granted speech. What followed was something that has forever changed me and spiked my faith to believe God's mercy for the miraculous. Not only did he stop screaming, but also he started to sleep at night. In addition, he started talking very rapidly and started to comprehend what was being said to Him. He started hitting the milestones so quickly that, by the time we got the appointment for autism evaluation, the doctor who had previously seen him said, "This is very unusual. Definitely not autism. If he were autistic, there is no way he could have made huge improvements within just months. His behavior and developmental delays were most likely caused by trauma."

Jelo continued to make huge strides, and when he turned three years old, he was admitted into specialized education preschool. Though he made tremendous amount of progress, it was recommended that he remain in specialized education as he was still behind in other areas. Within months, the head of that preschool said she wanted him in a regular classroom as he had completely closed the gap. He no longer benefitted being around children who were not the same level. The director of the preschool told me "I don't know what you have been doing, but one thing is for sure, this boy is not the same boy that he was when he first came here." He was put into a regular preschool classroom. The mercy of God exceeded my expectations. I started getting complains that Jelo talked too much in the classroom and on the bus. He wanted to tell everybody what to do; he was very chatty. I told them I thought that was a good problem for Jelo to have, and I promised to talk to him about it. The mercy of God can touch and heal your sick child. The mercy of God can help you conceive and deliver a healthy baby regardless of what the doctors may say. The mercy of God can make things better for you and your loved ones.

CHAPTER 4

LET MERCY STAND ALONE

The truth that I want you to grasp is this: Mercy accomplishes what long prayer and fasting and other kinds of seeking cannot. Mercy comes with no strings attached other than that we believe in it. Mercy is God's loving-kindness. It reaches into you to set you free. Initially there are no requirements that we must meet to receive mercy. Though, in order to ensure its continual supply in our lives, we must meet certain requirement as we shall see later in this book. This is because, when mercy comes upon us, we are no longer condemned and no longer judged. This is why God Himself instructed Moses to make the mercy seat on top of the Ark: "You shall put the mercy seat on top of the ark, and in the ark you shall put the Testimony that I will give you" (Exodus 25:21). Therefore, when God came to meet with his people, the first thing He saw was not commandments that they did not keep, but instead He saw the mercy seat. This is why also it is so important to ask for God's mercy and also expect it. Do not list your accomplishments or your good deeds when you need a miracle from God. They are not enough to satisfy God's righteousness.

All the things that the Bible admonishes us to do—giving, fasting and praying, teaching and preaching, taking care of the poor, going to church, loving our neighbors—are very important, and all those who consider themselves believers should run the race toward achieving those things. However, when we have failed to do any of those things or any other things that we are taught to do in the Word of God, we must remember not to pass judgment and sentence on ourselves. Yes, we deserve judgment, but we must always keep in mind that there is a mercy seat in heaven and that the One who sits on the throne at all times says, "Mercy triumphs over judgment!" And that mercy is available at no cost. Just ask for it and believe you will receive it!

MERCY BRINGS BLESSINGS TO YOUR LIFE

Sometimes we see people who, in our opinion, should not have been blessed with a level of possessions or achievements or success that is more than what we have been blessed with. (Keep in mind that a blessing could be any of the things that we have already talked about such as houses, cars, ministries, spouses, children, jobs, good health, businesses, great careers, ideas, and everything that you would consider important or valuable in life.) We think these people are probably not aligned with many of the right and good things that I have mentioned earlier such as great education, experience, giving, going to church, and loving their neighbor as they love themselves, but still they have all that you think you should have. This very topic came up just two days before I even knew that I would be writing a book about this subject. Looking back now, I know that God was preparing me for this.

One Saturday, I felt that I needed to visit an elderly lady whom I will call Jane, so I picked up the phone and called her. I asked her if she was going to be at home that afternoon, and she said yes. Then I asked her if it would be okay for me to visit with her. Without any hesitation she said yes. Since she lives not too far from where I live, I walked to her house. As soon as I got there, one of the very first things that she said was that one of the very prominent preachers on TV was struggling financially. If he didn't receive money soon, he would have to shut down his TV ministry. She continued to say, "I don't know why such a powerful minister would stop a TV ministry for lack of money. I know one preacher who really doesn't have any anointing, but he still has a TV ministry. And he has been on TV for a long time. I don't know how he can financially continue having a TV ministry."

When she was done expressing her disappointments, I told her that the mercy of God brings good things into our lives. Sometimes, this is not the result of what we do. Then I asked her if she knew anything about the story of Esau and Jacob. She said, "Not very much. Tell me about it."

I told her that, as she already knew, Isaac had two sons, Esau and Jacob. I went on to say that Esau represented what we would consider good people, believers or good Christians—people who seem to have their acts together and are talented, gifted, intelligent, educated, reliable, and highly skilled. They go to places of worship and do all the good things for proper and honorable living and what the Bible admonishes us to do like giving, serving, praying, forgiving, and loving. To the contrary, Jacob, as his name indicates, was a supplanter and did not represent what we would call good people, believers or good Christians in many ways. First of all, Jacob was not very dependable, and he was not a big giver. He was not very honest in many ways, and if those around him were not careful, he would take advantage of them. He did not volunteer for anything in the community or places of worship unless there was money involved to his advantage, and he did not like to work much either. In today's world, he would be called a mama's boy. He was the type of a person many of us would treat with caution. We would have him under a microscope twenty-four hours a day. The Bible says, "So the boys grew. And Esau was a skillful hunter, a man of the field; but Jacob was a mild man, dwelling in tents. And Isaac loved Esau because he ate of his game, but Rebekah loved Jacob" (Genesis 25:27–28).

In the scriptures, we are told that Jacob did not have skills like Esau did, and he did not do much either other than taking life as it came to him. He stayed home most of the time and did not go out often to take care of business as Esau did. Surprisingly, when it came to blessings, Jacob got the blessings, and Esau did not. Esau, like many of us, thought his way of life alone could qualify him to attain success and achieve prosperity, or blessings. (For us, in our world today, this would be giving, gaining a college education, making professional connections, working toward a great marriage, developing skills, and working hard.) He had no idea that a mild man like Jacob could go ahead of him and benefit for what he did not deserve. This is why the Bible says that God uses the weak to shame the wise: "But God has chosen the foolish things of the world to put to shame the wise, and God has chosen the weak things of the world to put to shame the things which are mighty" (1 Corinthians 1:27). Unfortunately, Esau learned about this principal very late, and there was nothing he could do to change the outcome; he just got angry. The Bible says, "So Esau hated Jacob because of the blessing with which his father blessed him, and Esau said in his heart, The days of mourning for my father are at hand; then I will kill my brother Jacob" (Mathew 27:41).

Esau tried to beg his father for any more blessing that he could have, but instead he was told that he should serve his brother. The Bible puts it this way:

> And Esau said to his father, "Have you only one blessing, my father? Bless me—me also, O my father!" And Esau lifted up his voice and wept. Then Isaac his father answered and said to him: "Behold, your dwelling shall be of the fatness of the earth, And of the dew of heaven from above. By your sword you shall live, And you shall serve your brother; *And* it shall come to pass, when you become restless, That you shall break his yoke from your neck." (Genesis 27:38–40)

Develop a Great Attitude toward God and His Mercy

Why did this happen to such a hardworking man? Esau believed that he deserved more than Jacob. He thought, as many of us think, that we deserve the success, prosperity, and all God's blessings because of our giving or our good deeds and for no other reason. Not so. Our knowledge of the nature of God is very important. Our attitude toward Him matters more than who we think we are, and certainly more than what we have done. God is holy and perfect. Most of the things He does for us have nothing to do with our so-called good deeds; rather, they have to do with who He is and our knowing and believing that He is merciful and that He wants to show mercy to us. As a matter of fact, He wants to show mercy to us, and He is waiting to show mercy to us: "Therefore the Lord will wait, that He may be gracious to you; And therefore He will be exalted, that He may have mercy on you. For the Lord *is* a God of justice; Blessed *are* all those who wait for Him" (Isaiah 30:18).

Jesus gave the example of two men who were praying at the temple. One of them boasted about his giving, and the other one was afraid even to look to heaven (in other words, he was humbled and feared the Lord). He beat his breast and asked for God's mercy. Jesus said that the latter was justified.

> Also, He spoke this parable to some who trusted in themselves that they were righteous, and despised others: "Two men went up to the temple to pray, one a Pharisee and the other a tax collector. The Pharisee stood and prayed

thus with himself, 'God, I thank You that I am not like other men—extortioners, unjust, adulterers, or even as this tax collector. I fast twice a week; I give tithes of all that I possess.' And the tax collector, standing afar off, would not so much as raise his eyes to heaven, but beat his breast, saying, 'God, be merciful to me a sinner!' I tell you, this man went down to his house justified rather than the other; for everyone who exalts himself will be humbled, and he who humbles himself will be exalted." (Luke 18:9–14)

Let's go back to the story of Esau. Like many of us, he said, "I have worked so hard for this and I deserve it." In other words, he had pride. And the Bible indicates clearly that God resists the proud and gives grace to the humble (1 Peter 5:5). Every time people like Esau pray, all they do is brag and tell God how much good they have done. I have had the privilege of being in prayer teams many times, and I have often witnessed this very thing. What comes out of people's mouths when they pray reveals their pride. Prayer should not be used to snub or correct others. The Bible says "Brood of vipers! How can you, being evil, speak good things? For out of the abundance of the heart the mouth speaks" (Mathew 12:34). This should teach us to watch what we say when we pray. It is very important for us to remember that none of us is good; only God is good. "Now a certain ruler asked Him, saying, 'Good Teacher, what shall I do to inherit eternal life?' So Jesus said to him, 'Why do you call Me good? No one is good but One, that is, God'" (Luke 18:18–19).

CHAPTER 5

BE WILLING TO LET GO OF
YOUR LITTLE THINGS

Esau believers forget that God is perfect and that the little things they do besides the anointing, attending church or places of worship, tithing, singing in a choir, being part of a worship team, preaching and teaching are not pleasing to Him. This is because, though Esau pleased his father in some ways, he still did things in his life that made life bitter for Isaac and Rebekah. This is recorded it this way: "When Esau was forty years old, he took as wives Judith the daughter of Beeri the Hittite, and Basemath the daughter of Elon the Hittite. And they were a grief of mind to Isaac and Rebekah" (Genesis 26:34–35).

God had clearly instructed the Jewish people not to marry idol worshippers. Esau married not just one idol worshipper but two idol worshippers. In addition to that, his wives were apparently troublemakers who brought a great deal of pain to Esau's parents. Esau's little thing was idol worshippers and troublemakers. He stirred up bad feelings and turmoil in his family. He caused a once quiet, peaceful, and tranquil family to experience agony.

Also, Esau did not know how important it was to deny the flesh and to yield to the will of God. In this case, he did not care about the value of his birthright. He was willing to trade it for a meal. For him, instant gratification was all that mattered: I want it, and I want it now. The Bible says that he despised his birthright. The book of Genesis tells this story this way:

> Now Jacob cooked a stew; and Esau came in from the field, and he was weary. And Esau said to Jacob, "Please feed me with that same red stew, for I am weary." Therefore his name was called Edom. But Jacob said, "Sell me your birthright as of this day." And Esau said, "Look, I am about to die; so what is this birthright to me?" Then Jacob said, "Swear to me as of this day." So he swore to him, and sold his birthright to Jacob. And Jacob gave Esau bread and stew of lentils; then he ate and drank, arose, and went his way. Thus Esau despised his birthright. (Genesis 25:29–34)

This should be taken as a cautionary tale from which we learn that the little things we do or say do matter a lot.

What you may consider not a big deal God may consider a big deal. Everything we do or say, God will remember. We must understand that what we do or say may negatively or positively impact our destinies for a very long time if not for a lifetime. Actions might be different for every person. For some, overspending could cause them to be in financial trouble all the time. For others, laziness could cause them to not have enough money to support themselves or their families. For still others, a little dishonesty, not giving faithfully, spreading misinformation, cheating, rebelling against parents, being jealous, lying, or discriminating against others could cause a variety of problems.

You may be tempted to think that much of this should not matter. However, this story was recorded in the Bible to tell us that those little things we do really matter. Our actions can work for us or against us. Yes, God wants to bypass our shortcomings and imperfections and grant us mercy; nevertheless, intentionally ignoring God's rules and commands will have you on the opposite side of mercy. That opposite side of mercy is judgement. God is holy, and He should be treated as such. It must be understood that shortcomings and imperfections are not the same thing as rebelling against the living God.

WHATEVER YOU ARE IGNORING TODAY WILL COST YOU TOMORROW

When I worked at a retail food company, management used to provide training in many different areas that related to our industry. They also provided training in the importance of eating well. One of the things they told us was, if you don't want to spend money now to buy healthy foods, you will spend money later in medical expenses. So, the issue is not *if* you should spend money but *when* you should spend money. In other words, pay now by buying healthful foods or pay later by buying drugs to treat diseases that are caused by bad diets. And this is how life is in many different ways. And this is the way it was with Esau. Days went by, and Esau ignored and probably forgot what he had done and what he had said. However, God did not ignore Esau's actions; neither did he forget them. When the day of blessings came, Jacob got the blessings and Esau did not. Genesis 27:1–29 records this story this way:

> Now it came to pass, when Isaac was old and his eyes were so dim that he could not see, that he called Esau his older son and said to him, 'My son.' And he answered him, "Here I am." Then he said, "Behold now, I am old. I do not know the day of my death. Now therefore, please take your weapons, your quiver and your bow, and go out to the field and hunt game for me. And make me savory food, such as I love, and bring it to me that I may eat, that my soul may bless you before I die." Now Rebekah was listening when Isaac spoke to Esau his son. And Esau went to the field to hunt game and to bring it. So Rebekah spoke to Jacob her son, saying, "Indeed I heard your

father speak to Esau your brother, saying, 'Bring me game and make savory food for me, that I may eat it and bless you in the presence of the Lord before my death.' Now therefore, my son, obey my voice according to what I command you. Go now to the flock and bring me from there two choice kids of the goats, and I will make savory food from them for your father, such as he loves. Then you shall take it to your father, that he may eat it, and that he may bless you before his death." And Jacob said to Rebekah his mother, "Look, Esau my brother is a hairy man, and I am a smooth-skinned man. Perhaps my father will feel me, and I shall seem to be a deceiver to him; and I shall bring a curse on myself and not a blessing." But his mother said to him, "Let your curse be on me, my son; only obey my voice, and go, get them for me." And he went and got them and brought them to his mother, and his mother made savory food, such as his father loved. Then Rebekah took the choice clothes of her elder son Esau, which were with her in the house, and put them on Jacob her younger son. And she put the skins of the kids of the goats on his hands and on the smooth part of his neck. Then she gave the savory food and the bread, which she had prepared, into the hand of her son Jacob. So he went to his father and said, "My father." And he said, "Here I am. Who are you, my son?" Jacob said to his father, "I am Esau your firstborn; I have done just as you told me; please arise, sit and eat of my game, that your soul may bless me." But Isaac said to his son, "How is it that you have found it so quickly, my son?" And he said, "Because the Lord your God brought it to me." Isaac said to Jacob, "Please come near, that I may feel you, my son, whether you are really my son Esau or not." So Jacob went near to Isaac his father, and he felt him and said, "The voice is Jacob's voice, but the hands are the hands of Esau." And he did not recognize him, because his hands were hairy like his brother Esau's hands; so he blessed him. Then he said, "Are you really my son Esau?" He said, "I am." He said, "Bring it near to me, and I will eat of my son's game, so that my soul may bless you." So he brought it near to him, and he ate; and he brought him wine, and he drank. Then his father Isaac said to him, "Come near now and kiss me, my son." And he came near and kissed him; and he smelled the smell of his clothing, and blessed him and said: "Surely, the smell of my son Is like the smell of a field Which the Lord has blessed. Therefore may God give you Of the dew of heaven, Of the fatness of the earth,

And plenty of grain and wine. Let peoples serve you, And nations bow down to you. Be master over your brethren, And let your mother's sons bow down to you. Cursed be everyone who curses you, And blessed be those who bless you!"

This is how Jacob believers are, and this is why, when it comes to blessings, they seem to be getting ahead and getting away with everything in comparison to what the Esau believers are receiving. But we must remember that the merciful God determines our success. Though having a good education and being intelligent are very important, they are not the only things that guarantee high achievement. Mercy is the ingredient that makes the difference. And the merciful God not only looks at what we do and say, but he also considers the attitudes of our hearts and why we say and do certain things. Matters of the heart are very important to God. You can see the parallels between Esau and Jacob. Esau never cared about the consequences of his actions or words and neither did he seem to worry about it. When his two wives caused grief to his mother and father, he didn't seem to take any action to rectify the situation. In addition, when he was hungry and Jacob told him to sell him his birthright, he didn't think clearly either. All he said was, "Look, I am about to die, so what is this birthright to me?" It didn't end there. Esau had a chance to change his mind and say, "This is not a good idea. Forget about the stew. I am not going to sell you my birthright. No way, supplanter." Sadly he didn't. That gave Jacob more tenacity to advance his proposal, and Esau fell for it easily. The story is narrated in Genesis 25:31–34 this way: "Then Jacob said, 'Swear to me as of this day.' So he swore to him, and sold his birthright to Jacob. And Jacob gave Esau bread and stew of lentils; then he ate and drank, arose, and went his way. Thus Esau despised his birthright."

Tragically, like most people, in his mind Esau thought, *It is really not a big deal. There is no witness. No one heard us, and no one saw us. Jacob is ridiculous to think that he can get something out of this without a written agreement. I am going to go on my way as if the conversation we had never really happened. I was never there.* Esau forgot that God is a covenant keeper and that He was a witness of that verbal agreement. He was there. He saw and heard it, and He would see to it that Jacob got his mercy and justice when the time came. The Bible says this:

> "I have loved you," says the Lord. But you say, "How have you loved us?" "Is not Esau Jacob's brother?" declares the Lord. "Yet I have loved Jacob but Esau I have hated. I have laid waste his hill country and left his heritage to jackals of the desert." (Malachi 1:2–3)

The sovereignty of God and His omnipresence enabled Him to witness what was said and done between the two brothers. It does not seem that either their father, Isaac, or their mother, Rebekah, knew of that verbal transaction between their two sons; nevertheless, that did not deter nor hinder God from orchestrating a perfect circumstance to make sure Jacob got what he had bought from Esau, his brother. The Bible says that Rebekah had overheard Isaac telling Esau to prepare the meal before he was blessed. What are the chances that Rebekah wouldn't have been there at that moment to overhear that conversation? She could have been anywhere else—outside, taking a nap, or visiting someone at that very moment. However, the Lord God Almighty in His sovereignty made sure that she was there at that very moment to capture that important piece of information that would change the course history of her two sons. Also, Jacob seemed not to be too far from home that day either. If Jacob had been traveling that day and not at home, he would not have been able to be blessed even though his mother was there and wanted to help him to get the blessing. It took people being at the right place and at the right time to capture the blessing. The mercy of God had made it possible for all of that to happen.

Why did Jacob attract the mercy of God instead of brother, Esau? Jacob's heart was in a right place, and he demonstrated a cautious heart because he did not want to grieve his dad. In Genesis 27:11–15, we read the following text:

> And Jacob said to Rebekah his mother, "Look, Esau my brother is a hairy man, and I am a smooth-skinned man. Perhaps my father will feel me, and I shall seem to be a deceiver to him; and I shall bring a curse on myself and not a blessing." But his mother said to him, "Let your curse be on me, my son; only obey my voice, and go, get them for me." And he went and got

them and brought them to his mother, and his mother made savory food, such as his father loved.

Jacob desired to do things right to the best of his ability. He was not as reckless as Esau was.

GET RID OF ANYTHING THAT MAY HINDER YOUR MERCY AND BLESSINGS

This story should not only teach us about mercy; it should also teach us that there are things that we do or say that block every possible blessing from coming our way. Because of that, we can miss out on God's best blessings for our lives. Because of his attitude, his actions and his words, Esau lost his blessings this way:

> Now it happened, as soon as Isaac had finished blessing Jacob, and Jacob had scarcely gone out from the presence of Isaac his father, that Esau his brother came in from his hunting. He also had made savory food, and brought it to his father, and said to his father, "Let my father arise and eat of his son's game, that your soul may bless me." And his father Isaac said to him, "Who are you?" So he said, "I am your son, your firstborn, Esau." Then Isaac trembled exceedingly, and said, "Who? Where is the one who hunted game and brought it to

me? I ate all of it before you came, and I have blessed him—and indeed he shall be blessed." When Esau heard the words of his father, he cried with an exceedingly great and bitter cry, and said to his father, "Bless me—me also, O my father!" But he said, "Your brother came with deceit and has taken away your blessing." And Esau said, "Is he not rightly named Jacob? For he has supplanted me these two times. He took away my birthright, and now look, he has taken away my blessing!" And he said, "Have you not reserved a blessing for me?" Then Isaac answered and said to Esau, "Indeed I have made him your master, and all his brethren I have given to him as servants; with grain and wine I have sustained him. What shall I do now for you, my son?" And Esau said to his father, "Have you only one blessing, my father? Bless me—me also, O my father!" And Esau lifted up his voice and wept. Then Isaac his father answered and said to him: " Behold, your dwelling shall be of the fatness of the earth, And of the dew of heaven from above. By your sword you shall live, And you shall serve your brother; And it shall come to pass, when you become restless, That you shall break his yoke from your neck." (Genesis 27:30–40)

Not only did his attitude and his words hinder blessings; they hindered mercy too. The Bible tells us that, when Esau wanted the blessings, he could not get them though he sought them with tears: "Lest there be any fornicator or profane person like Esau, who for one morsel of food sold his birthright. For you know that afterward, when he wanted to inherit the blessing, he was rejected, for he found no place for repentance, though he sought it diligently with tears" (Hebrews 12:16–18).

RIGHT MOTIVES MAKE A DIFFERENCE

Jacob, in contrast to Esau, though he was not as hard working as Esau in his father's eyes, did not make his parents bitter. This means that he cared for his father's opinion in the most crucial matters in his life. Though he didn't do a lot of things that were right in his father's sight (including pretending that he was Esau in order to get the blessings), he had the correct motive for what he did. And the best part of all, he feared his dad.

Do you fear your Father who is in heaven? Do you have the correct motive for things you do and say? Do you care about your heavenly Father's opinion of you and his wishes about what you should and should not do? Is the will of God the most important thing in your life? The right answers to these questions will open new doors of blessings that you never knew existed. If you do not have the right answers now, it is not too late, for the door is still open. I must make it clear that the difference between you and Esau is that you do have an opportunity to make this a new day. You can ask God for forgiveness. He desires to show you mercy. And after you do that, come boldly to Him and plead for mercy as the Bible says: "Let us therefore come boldly to the throne of grace, that we may obtain mercy and find grace to help in time of need" (Hebrews 4:16).

It is not too late. God is truly a God of mercy, and His mercy is unfailing.

CHAPTER 6

TRUST IN GOD'S MERCY, NOT YOUR ABILITIES

I had just walked into a new office on my first day at a new job, my first position as a finance manager since I had graduated from college. I had "classroom knowledge" of how to do the job but no experience. It was a competitive position, and by the mercy of God, I had been the successful candidate and had been offered the job. I looked around my new office. It had just been furnished with a new chair, desk, and file cabinet. On top of that desk was a brand-new laptop. I sat down, opened the computer, and saw that the accounting software was already installed. I would use this software to manage the finances of the organization.

A few days prior to starting that job, I had a conversation with the Lord in which I told Him that I would not be able to do the job that He had given me unless he helped me. I asked Him to be merciful to me and grant me success. I expressed my deepest fears about my new position; honestly, I was really scared.

I explored the unused accounting software, and I started working. My new boss brought in a bunch of documents that needed to be structured, entered, and posted. I was able to generate some documents my boss requested. When I took the documents to him, he asked me to clarify what I had presented to him. My answer was "I don't know." Yes, I told him I didn't know. For some reason, he was not angry with me for that answer, but he was surprised. He said, "Go and come back." I left his office and went back to my office. When I got to my office, I reminded God that, unless He helped me, I would be hugely embarrassed to have failed in the job that He had given me over many other candidates who were more experienced than I. I pleaded for His mercy. I don't remember exactly how and when the shift in my ability to perform with excellency in that position came, but one thing I remember vividly is that my boss promoted me to another position after I had done so well in that first position. He put me in charge of training another new graduate who had just been hired for my previous position. When the organization hired an agency to do the audit at the end of the financial year, the agency representative said that it was the first time he had done an audit in a new department without finding errors. The board of directors were thrilled and amazed by the reports. When my boss saw that I was also making huge strides in the second position he had given me, he said, "When you first started working here, you used to tell me 'I don't know' when you presented your work. Then suddenly everything changed, and you exceeded my expectations. You have also turned around this new position that you have. You are very talented."

I knew it was the mercy of God that had helped me. His loving-kindness not only enabled me to keep my position and succeed in it, but also enabled me to bring financial success to the organization, and that made my boss look and feel really good. That's a mystery of the mercies of God. When God shows mercy on someone, it impacts even those around them. What makes the mercy of God so profound is that it has no limits. You can ask for anything. This is because God is omniscient; he has complete and unlimited knowledge, awareness, and understanding. He is also all powerful. His mercies can take care every detail of our lives—health, marriage, business, family, addictions, relationships, disabilities, and education. Mercy enables us to access the kingdom of God. The kingdom of God has all the provisions that we need. When we approach God on the basis of mercy, we tap into the sufficiency of His kingdom. There is sufficiency in the kingdom of God. Also, His kingdom rules over everything that you can think of. His kingdom rules over all. Psalm 103:19 says, "The Lord has established His throne in heaven, And His kingdom rules over all."

King David, one of the greatest kings in Israel, understood the principle of trusting God's mercy and not his ability. It is no wonder he was able to be the greatest king that Israel has ever known. It is because he did not depend on his anointing alone to defeat his enemies. He trusted in God's mercy and not his abilities. Here is what David said:

7The righteous also shall see and fear, And shall laugh at him, saying, "Here is the man who did not make God his strength, But trusted in the abundance of his riches, And strengthened himself in his wickedness." But I am like a green olive tree in the house of God; I trust in the mercy of God forever and ever. I will praise You forever, Because You have done it; And in the presence of Your saints. I will wait on Your name, for it is good. (Psalm 52:6–9).

This is why David was able to defeat Goliath when he was just a youth. When Goliath came to him all prepared and appearing strong and professional, David was not moved; instead, he announced the death of Goliath with heavy convictions in the name of the Lord. Bystanders and his brothers tried to remind him that he was not qualified to fight the giant, but he insisted that there was a cause, which means there was a need, and he proceeded. In 1 Samuel 17:45–50, we read:

Then David said to the Philistine, "You come to me with a sword, with a spear, and with a javelin. But I come to you in the name of the Lord of hosts, the God of the armies of Israel, whom you have defied. This day the Lord will deliver you into my hand, and I will strike you and take your head from you. And this day I will give the carcasses of the camp of the Philistines to the birds of the air and the wild beasts of the earth, that all the earth may know that there is a God in Israel. Then all this assembly shall know that the Lord does not save with sword and spear; for the battle *is* the Lord, and He will give you into our hands." So it was, when the Philistine arose and came and drew near to meet David, that David hurried and ran toward the army to meet the Philistine. Then David put his hand in his bag and took out a stone; and he slung *it* and struck the Philistine in his forehead, so that the stone sank into his forehead, and he fell on his face to the earth. So David prevailed over the Philistine with a sling and a stone, and struck the Philistine and killed him. But *there was* no sword in the hand of David. (1 Samuel 17:45–50)

God's mercy is a secret weapon we can use to destroy every giant that comes our way. Our credentials are very limited; we are not qualified in all areas of life, but the power of God's mercy is unlimited. Know it, acknowledge it, and let it work in your life and in the lives of those you love, your ministry, your career, your dreams, and your visions. Keep in mind that, when mercy comes in your circumstance or situation, it qualifies you to be a champion.

King David knew this secret power of mercy, and this is why he trusted in it. He even asked for God's mercy to come early sometimes. How could he possibly do that? The answer is that he knew the power of mercy. He said, "Oh, satisfy us early with Your mercy, That we may rejoice and be glad all our days!" (Psalm 90:14).

When the mercy of God comes upon you, you shall rejoice and be glad all of your days. May the Lord God of Abraham, Isaac, and Jacob help us to understand the magnitude of His mercy in our lives.

CHAPTER 7

WHO QUALIFIES FOR MERCY?

> For He says to Moses, "I will have mercy
> on whomever I will have mercy, and I will
> have compassion on whomever I will have
> compassion." So then it is not of him who
> wills, nor of him who runs, but of God who
> shows mercy. (Romans 9:15–16)

Who qualifies for mercy? The answer may surprise you:
anyone! Yes, anyone who is alive qualifies for mercy as long
as he or she knows how to ask for it. This is where I have
a problem with religious people who think that their good
works qualify them for a lot of things if not all things.
But this book was not written for religious people; instead,
it was written for God's people. Again, as long as people

can acknowledge God and who He is, they can ask for mercy and receive it. According to the Word of God, people from all walks of life came to the Lord and asked Him to have mercy on them, and He did. You too can do that. Just believe! The Canaanite woman who today would be classified as an unbeliever was able to obtain mercy from God, and her daughter was cured from demon possession because her mother cried out for mercy.

BE PERSISTENT AND DETERMINED WHEN ASKING FOR MERCY

Persistence is very important when asking God for mercy. Not receiving the answer or a response to your first cry of mercy does not mean you have been rejected. You must continue with faith in your asking for mercy with the assurance that not only is God able to grant you mercy, but He also watches and waits because He wants to grant you mercy. The Canaanite woman had not only the faith that her request would be granted, but she also had the persistence and determination to not give up until she got the answer she wanted. Let us revisit the passage as it is written Matthew 15:21–28:

> Then Jesus went out from there and departed to the region of Tyre and Sidon. And behold, a woman of Canaan came from that region and cried out to Him, saying, "Have mercy on me, O Lord, Son

of David! My daughter is severely demon-possessed." But He answered her not a word. And His disciples came and urged Him, saying, "Send her away, for she cries out after us." But He answered and said, "I was not sent except to the lost sheep of the house of Israel." Then she came and worshiped Him, saying, "Lord, help me!" But He answered and said, "It is not good to take the children's bread and throw *it* to the little dogs." And she said, "Yes, Lord, yet even the little dogs eat the crumbs which fall from their masters' table." Then Jesus answered and said to her, "O woman, great *is* your faith! Let it be to you as you desire." And her daughter was healed from that very hour.

The problem that causes most people to be unable to see results after they ask God for mercy is that they give up too soon. They interpret the delay to their request for mercy as rejection. You must maintain the attitude of not being offended by God just because He didn't answer your prayer at the specific time that you wanted Him to. Let the Canaanite woman inspire you to press on with your asking for mercy till you get results. Other people may become annoyed by the same prayer request as the disciples did when the woman kept following Jesus and asking for mercy, but Jesus was not annoyed. That shows that God is not annoyed with your persistence when you ask for mercy. Keep in mind that God is more patient than any person.

LET FAITH ACCOMPANY YOUR REQUEST FOR MERCY

Keep in mind that mercy eliminates any demands (except for faith) or requirements you must meet to receive what you need. When you get a revelation of what mercy really is, you will not wait until you get it all together to receive miracles, deliverance, and blessings that you have been waiting for. You just need to show faith while asking for mercy.

YOU DON'T HAVE TO GET IT ALL TOGETHER TO ASK FOR MERCY

Just come as you are. When Jesus was on this earth, many people—believers (those who believe in God) and unbelievers (those who do not believe in God)—came to Him with their requests for mercy. The most exciting thing is that He granted their requests.

And that is why the Bible depicts the story of the Canaanite woman who went to Jesus to ask for healing for her daughter who was severely demon possessed in a detailed and profound way. This woman was not a believer; in other words, she was not religious. In short, she did not worship God of Abraham, Isaac and Jacob, God of Israel; she was not saved, neither was she a born-again Christian. And even Jesus Himself tried to talk her out of asking for mercy for her daughter by pointing out that she was not a believer. Surprisingly, the woman did not deny that she was not a believer; neither did she try to be defensive about why she was not a believer. Instead, she continued with her request for mercy until it was granted. She was unstoppable. In the end, she received a miracle. Yes, you may still be struggling with addictions, unfaithfulness, and a bunch of other life problems. You are still a good candidate for God's mercy.

For many of us, encountering the storms of life and having little or no time to get things together with God should be a life learning experience. We need to ask for God's mercy to intervene. There are times when we will not have time or resources to sow a seed and reap a harvest; however, we will always have a chance to exercise our faith and ask for God's mercy. This does not mean that sowing seeds is not important; indeed, the Bible states it very clearly: "While the earth remains, Seedtime and harvest, Cold and heat, Winter and summer, And day and night Shall not cease" (Genesis 8:22).

Moreover, what is being said here is that mercy will accomplish what other good deeds cannot. This is why, when this woman pleaded for mercy, Jesus did not demand that she be a believer first (though He pointed out that she was not). He just allowed mercy to intervene. So many times, we get caught up in the religious mentality of explaining why this prayer or that prayer was not answered. Sometimes we even try to explain why some people have not received their miracles or have not been blessed in this or that, while the only question that we need to ask sometimes is Have we, or have they, prayed for mercy?

RESIST THE TEMPTATION TO HAVE A PITY PARTY

We must also keep in mind that asking for mercy is not the same as asking for God to feel sorry for us. We are not seeking God's sympathy; instead, we are seeking God's loving-kindness. You are seeking for God to give you help and to have compassion for you. I believe this is why the woman we just read about did not have a pity party immediately when Jesus challenged her request. Also, she did not even appear to be offended or insulted. She knew that she did not deserve anything from Jesus but mercy—not even sympathy. Anyone can have sympathy for you even when he or she is not able to do anything about your situation. However, mercy is different. We ask for mercy from people who have authority to do something about our situations, and these are the people who are able to provide the mercy we need. She was relentless with her request until she got what she needed. She did not say, "Maybe if I become converted things will go my way. Or maybe if I go to His synagogue this Saturday or church this Sunday, He will pray for my daughter." All she did was continue to stand on the unshakable ground of mercy. Not too long afterward, mercy showed up, and her misery was history. The miracle became hers to be held.

WHEN YOU NEED MERCY, CONDEMNING YOURSELF IS A BAD IDEA

The problem with many of us is that we condemn ourselves too soon, too much, and we stop believing we deserve mercy. And when we get into this condemnation trap, we lose our confidence before God, and we don't believe we are the right candidate for mercy. The Bible says, "Beloved, if our heart does not condemn us, we have confidence toward God" (1 John 3:21).

Condemnation takes away confidence. And once you lose confidence, you lose your ability to stand firm almost toward anything. This does not mean that we deny our shortcomings or defend our imperfections; rather, it means that we acknowledge our shortcomings and keep on asking for mercy from God who is whole, perfect, and complete.

MERCY APPLIES TO EVERY AREA OF YOUR LIFE

You are probably reading this book while you are in a solitary confinement or a prison somewhere. For some people it is a physical prison, and for some it is an emotional, psychological, relational, mental or financial prison. You may even think that this does not apply to you based on what you have done or how long life has been the way it is. Today I want to tell you this: When you have learned about the mercy of God, cry out for it. Ask for it, and the Lord God Almighty will hear you and grant you mercy. Take a step of faith and do what is right by asking God for mercy for your situation. He will answer you as He has answered many who came before. God does not show favoritism to anyone as people do. "Then Peter opened *his* mouth and said: "In truth I perceive that God shows no partiality. But in every nation whoever fears Him and works righteousness is accepted by Him" (Acts 10:34–35).

Nevertheless, God accepts every request of mercy from anyone who acknowledges it and asks for it. And, yes, it is true that mercy applies to your situation too.

MERCY HEALS SICKNESSES
AND DISEASES

Jesus healed all the people who came to Him with sicknesses and diseases and cried out for mercy regardless of their shortcomings. Maybe you are a parent who has a child with a debilitating disease or a child who is just out control in some way. Or maybe you need physical healing yourself. You can ask for mercy in these situations. We previously read the story in the Bible about a man who went to Jesus with a request about his son. His son was epileptic and suffered in many ways. Prior to his visit to Jesus, the father had gone to prayer meetings seeking help for his son, but he had been unsuccessful. His final hope was his plea for mercy. When mercy intervened, his son was cured. The Bible tells the story this way:

> And when they had come to the multitude, a man came to Him, kneeling down to Him and saying, "Lord, have mercy on my son, for he is an epileptic and suffers severely; for he often falls into the fire and often into the water. So I brought him to Your disciples, but they could not cure him." Then Jesus answered and said, "O faithless and perverse generation, how long shall I be with you? How long shall I bear with you? Bring him here to Me." And Jesus rebuked the demon, and it came out of him; and the child was cured from that very hour." (Mathew 17:14–18)

You may say "Mhm, this man may have had other issues in his faith, and that is why he did not receive help for his son immediately." You are probably right, but the bottom line is this: He cried out for mercy this time, and his son was set free.

CHAPTER 8

ASK FOR MERCY THAT YOUR SPIRITUAL EYES MIGHT BE OPENED

Asking for mercy is not only for physical or emotional life; it is also for spiritual life too. It is important to have our spiritual eyes opened or enlightened so we can know just what has been given to us.

> That the God of our Lord Jesus Christ, the Father of glory, may give to you the spirit of wisdom and revelation in the knowledge of Him, the eyes of your understanding being enlightened; that you may know what is the hope of His calling, what are the riches of the glory of His inheritance in the saints. (Ephesians 1:17–18)

I do not know about you, but I've lived my life as a Christian. Even so, I was so blind to many spiritual things. And I will tell you this: It is better to have spiritual eyes that can see those things that are hidden to many. We tend to think that, just because we have been believers or Christians for many years, perhaps have attended seminary or Bible college and have become pastors, rabbis, and teachers we know more of God's truth and have more revelation. That is one of the biggest lies that Satan loves to make people believe. It is one of the biggest deceptions that sweep away God's people, ministries, and churches. Just because you have done all those things that people in your position are expected to do to be effective, so to speak, it does not necessarily follow that you are spiritually in tune.

This reminds me of an evangelist I met while visiting a particular bookstore; I will call him Mark. I had just picked a book from the shelf and wanted to sit and read, and I chose a chair at the table where Mark was working. A few minutes after I sat down, I noticed that he had placed a few books on the table along with a Bible, and he seemed to be very busy with whatever he was doing. For some reason, I was compelled to say something to him, so I said, "Is that the Bible?" He said it was. I went on and asked him if he was preparing a message and if he was a Christian. He answered yes again. At this point, he stopped what was he was doing and asked me if I was a Christian too. I told him I was. Not too long after this initial meeting, I learned that he had been an evangelist for eight years and had been very successful in his work as a minister of the gospel, which he had been doing for three years at the time that we met at the bookstore. As we were talking, I learned that his ministry had gone from hundreds to tens, and he had been mentally, physically, and emotionally ruined by the enemy. As he was talking to me, there were moments when he stopped and wept. Keep in mind that I had just met him. After six hours of conversation, I learned that it had been a while since he had experienced a good night's sleep, and sometimes he would get so confused that he couldn't remember where he lived. There were moments when he could not talk very well; it seemed as if his mind wandered off somewhere. He described the experience as one of feeling blank. To make a long story short, I opened the Bible and shared some scriptures among which was this one:

> Put on the whole armor of God that you may be able to stand against the wiles of the devil. For we do not wrestle against flesh and blood, but against principalities, against powers, against the rulers of the darkness of this age, against spiritual hosts of wickedness in the heavenly places. (Ephesians 6:11–12)

And you know what is interesting? He knew almost the entire Bible, and he was able to tell me exactly where that scripture was without using a concordance. He knew many verses by heart. However, he could not sleep, and his mind was going blank. He had scriptures in his mind, but he did not have the truth of the scriptures in his heart. He had eyes but could not see. And since his theology did not seem to help him, he needed the mercy of God to help him see. I took advantage of the opportunity, and I introduced him to mercy. The Bible speaks about two blind men who had eyes, but their eyes were shut, and they could not see. The good thing for these two blind men was that they knew they had a problem that needed to be fixed. Being blind is one thing and recognizing that you are blind is another. This is how the Bible tells the story:

> Now as they went out of Jericho, a great multitude followed Him. And behold, two blind men sitting by the road, when they heard that Jesus was passing by, cried out, saying, "Have mercy on us, O Lord, Son of David!" Then the multitude warned them that they should be quiet; but they cried out all the more, saying, "Have mercy on us, O Lord, Son of David!" So Jesus stood still and called them, and said, "What do you want Me to do for you?" They said to Him, "Lord, that our eyes may be opened." So Jesus had compassion and touched their eyes. And immediately their eyes received sight, and they followed Him" (Mathew 20:29–34).

This tells us that we can have eyes and still not be able to see. We could memorize the Bible from cover to cover and still not be able to understand and apply the messages in our lives. We need our eyes to be opened. We need enlightened spiritual eyes to see what God has already given us. This is very important. Without this, the enemy can and will easily steal what belongs to us. Too much knowledge of the Bible by itself without enlightened eyes will not get you anywhere. Too many people spend so much time and many years going from one Bible study to another. Some people obtain multiple theology degrees. However, the problem still remains, and in some cases, it increases in time because they know too much intellectually, but this knowledge cannot help them to advance spiritually or to help someone else.

What you have learned so far should get you out of trouble and enable you to experience undeniable growth—if you have your spiritual eyes open. All you need is open eyes that can see. You must be enlightened. And once you are enlightened, you will be just fine. You do not need additional teaching to be effective. What you need is the revelation of the Holy Spirit or illumination from God to bring what you already know to life.

Remember Mark, the minister I met at the bookstore? Today he is not the same. He was healed miraculously, and his mind and emotional state have been restored completely. The message was very simple: You need mercy. Though he had a more knowledge of the Bible than most people I know, he needed mercy from God to get him out of the trouble he was in. He did not need any more sermons about deliverance; rather, he needed his eyes to be enlightened. He also needed to know where his good deeds end and where God's mercy starts. Did he pray by himself alone? No. A few days after I met him, I asked another person to join him and me. Together we asked for God's mercy on his behalf so he might be healed. And he was. See this as an invitation for you to come to God today and ask Him for mercy. He will grant it to you.

I must not overemphasize how important it is for our eyes to be open. I believe this is because so many of us tend to wander from place to place looking for God's best for us. We do not know that what we need is right in front of us. The Bible speaks of how Ishmael's life and that of his mother, Hagar, were sustained after Sarah (Abraham's wife) wanted them out her family. Hagar needed water after she had used up the water she had. She did not know what to do; she believed that she and her son were going to die because they did not have anything to drink. After she made that conclusion, she simply wept. The entire time she was having negative thoughts and believing she and her son would die, the well of water was right in front of her. However, she could not see the well until her eyes were opened; in other words, she was enlightened.

> And the water in the skin was used up, and she placed the boy under one of the shrubs. Then she went and sat down across from him at a distance of about a bowshot; for she said to herself, "Let me not see the death of the boy." So she sat opposite him, and lifted her voice and wept. And God heard the voice of the lad. Then the angel of God called to Hagar out of heaven, and said to her, "What ails you, Hagar? Fear not, for God has heard the voice of the lad where he is. Arise, lift up the lad and hold him with your hand, for I will make him a great nation." Then God opened her eyes, and she saw a well of water. And she went

and filled the skin with water, and gave the lad a drink. So God was with the lad; and he grew and dwelt in the wilderness, and became an archer. (Genesis 21:15–20)

Could it be that what you have been looking for, praying for, dreaming about, and waiting for is right in front you? Wouldn't you be happy if you could just see what has already been provided for you? Remember, you cannot see unless the eyes of your understanding have been enlightened. This is why it is more than crucial to have our eyes opened if we really want God to be known in our lives in a personal way so He may prosper us in every way. Moreover, we must remember that, before we make negative conclusions about our situations or circumstances, our eyes have to be enlightened enough to see the truth of the matter; in other words, to see things as God sees them. This is because most of the time what we see, is not what God sees. We see death, God sees life.

CHAPTER 9

HAVE MERCY ON OTHERS SO YOU CAN RECEIVE MERCY FOR YOURSELF

Blessed are the merciful, for they shall receive mercy. (Mathew 5:7)

Now that we have learned the importance of mercy and what it does for those who receive it, we must also learn the important element that opens doors through which mercy flows. Mathew 5:7 is the only verse in the Bible that clearly describes this important element of obtaining mercy. In simple language it means that, if we give mercy to others, we will receive mercy for ourselves. There is no other way around.

This means that, every day in our lives, we are given opportunities to have mercy on others in different ways and levels. We are also given opportunities to receive mercy from others. Nevertheless, the choice is ours. The continual supply of mercy in our lives depends on how much mercy we extend to others on a daily basis. This is where attitudes must be adjusted, especially for a lot of people who live in a culture that believes that you get what you pay for—no more, no less. However, with the principle of mercy, it does not have to be this way. With the principle of mercy, we give people what mercy has to offer at its best rather than giving people what we believe they deserve. If we do the opposite, we suffer loss of mercy ourselves. Then we go about our business and get what we deserve too. We end up frustrated, bitter, and depressed. We forget the principle of sowing and reaping. We fail to put into action one of Jesus's commandments: "Therefore, whatever you want men to do to you, do also to them, for this is the Law and the Prophets" (Mathew 7:12).

It is important to remember that you are going to need mercy from both God and people. This is why the Bible says, "This being so, I myself always strive to have a conscience without offense toward God and men" (Acts 24:16).

It is a foolish thing to think that, just because you have a good standing with God, you do not need to have a good standing with people. Both God and people are important as far as the issue of mercy is concerned. We must create an atmosphere in which we will attract mercy into our lives continuously. This is not an easy thing to do since it requires giving of ourselves to make life better for others. Why? Because mercy is giving others what they do not deserve. It is giving people what profits them rather than practicing judgment and condemnation. It is accepting inconveniences at times to make life convenient for others.

The importance of extending mercy to others cannot be overstated. This is why Jesus emphasized it to His disciples on more than one occasion. Even when Peter asked Him how many times he was supposed to be kind and compassionate with people, Jesus responded seventy times seven, which meant countless times. Jesus continued to put emphasis on his message of the importance of giving mercy to others in order to receive mercy for ourselves as recorded in Matthew 18:23–35:

> Therefore the kingdom of heaven is like a certain king who wanted to settle accounts with his servants. And when he had begun to settle accounts, one was brought to him who owed him ten thousand talents. But as he was not able to pay, his master commanded that he be sold, with his wife and children and all that he had, and that payment be made. The servant therefore fell down before him, saying, 'Master, have patience with me, and I will pay you all.' Then the master of that servant was moved with compassion, released him, and forgave him the debt. "But that servant went out and found one of his fellow servants who owed him a hundred denarii; and he laid hands on him and took *him* by the throat, saying, 'Pay me what you owe!' So his fellow servant fell down at his feet and

begged him, saying, 'Have patience with me, and I will pay you all.' And he would not, but went and threw him into prison till he should pay the debt. So when his fellow servants saw what had been done, they were very grieved, and came and told their master all that had been done. Then his master, after he had called him, said to him, 'You wicked servant! I forgave you all that debt because you begged me. Should you not also have had compassion on your fellow servant, just as I had pity on you?' And his master was angry, and delivered him to the torturers until he should pay all that was due to him. "So My heavenly Father also will do to you if each of you, from his heart, does not forgive his brother his trespasses."

How tragic that the unmerciful servant thought he could receive mercy but did not have any responsibility to extend mercy to others. Unfortunately, this is the thinking of many of us today. We take and take, but we barely give. Let this be the siren that gets our attention and compels us to be intentional in extending mercy to others. What is so fascinating with this parable of the unmerciful servant is that he was shown mercy for a much bigger debt than the one his fellow servant had accrued. The story shows how our self-centeredness tends to inflate the mistakes of others and minimize our own.

This is one of the difficult things I have had to confront

in my own life. Years ago, I went through a phase in which I was disobedient to the Lord multiple times. This led me to make several bad choices that resulted in big losses in almost all areas of my life, including dear friendships. I was left with nothing. I later recognized my mistakes. I repented and asked the Lord to have mercy on me and restore me and all that I had lost. God started to make good things happen for me, and the rebuilding of my life began. I didn't have everything, but I was in a good place at the time.

Consequently, during this time of restoration, I made a new friend I will call Bella. Bella and I became good friend, or so I thought. She was financially better off than I was at the time. We became prayer partners too and did lots of things together. During the course of our friendship, she supposedly made another friend whom I will call Nancy. I knew Nancy from church, and I knew she was a wealthy woman. Bella and Nancy became very close, and Bella started ignoring me. It came to the point that I couldn't plan anything with Bella because her activities were subject to change if Nancy called her even half an hour prior to Bella's plans with me. Bella didn't want much to do with me anymore except for when she needed something from me. One incident finally made me reconsider my friendship with Bella. On Passover morning after church, I was preparing the table for a meal. I had invited Bella and another friend a few weeks before that, and Bella had accepted my invitation. When she arrived, she told me "I am going to eat quickly and leave because I have plans with Nancy today." She quickly ate, and with no apology, left the Passover meal. I was hurt. I chose to enjoy the rest of the meal with my other friend. Later, when Bella reached out to see what I was up to, I told her that I didn't appreciate the way our relationship had been going lately, and I wanted to take a break from our friendship. She didn't apologize; instead, she was defensive and tried to manipulate me into thinking that I was just creating something out of nothing. I chose not to doubt my reality. I continued with my life and pursued other relationships.

A few months later, Bella came to me in tears and told me that she and Nancy were no longer friends. She stated that Nancy had exploded on her one day and told her that she didn't want to be friends with her anymore because she was so needy. Apparently, Bella kept asking Nancy for things, and Nancy couldn't support Bella's neediness anymore. It didn't surprise me as I had still been attending church with both of these women. What Bella didn't know was that Nancy had called me and told me how she appreciated me for who I was. She told me that she was tired of fake friends from church who followed her and wanted to be friends with her only because she was rich and her children were millionaires. She said, "You don't ask me for anything." So when Bella lamented that she had been rejected by Nancy, I did a good job keeping my mouth shut. I was so glad neither of these women were my friends, and I said to myself, *I'm not going to be friends with Bella again because of the way she treated me when she was friends with Nancy.*

A few weeks after Bella told me about the end of her friendship with Nancy, she called me and said she was sick and she was going to have surgery. She told me that she didn't have anyone to drive her to and from the hospital. I am ashamed to admit that I was tempted to tell her that I was very busy, and I didn't want anything to do with her. Thankfully, I did not yield to that temptation because the Holy Spirit was quick to point it out to me that mercy triumphs over judgement. Somehow, that struck a chord in me, and I remembered the amount of help I received from all kinds of people when I lost everything. I remembered how I had been taken care of and how I hadn't lacked anything. I remembered how even total strangers had come to my aid in my time of need. I yielded to what the Holy Spirit had made clear to me, which was not only to drive Bella to the hospital to get her surgery done but also to make sure I tended to her till she recovered. I asked Bella for the details of her appointment so I could plan to take her. I said nothing about how disappointed and hurt I had been when she discarded me for her new friend. I took a day off from work and drove my old friend who had discarded me for a rich friend to the hospital. I spent the next few days tending to her and making sure she has fully recovered. After she recovered, she said, "Caster, you are Jesus's hands and feet. You took care of me." I was humbled. For the first time, it also deeply dawned on me what Jesus had meant when he said, "Let your light so shine before men, that they may see your good works and glorify your Father in heaven" (Matthew 15:16).

This experience has changed the way I deal with people regardless of what they have done to me or of how I feel about them. I have come to realize that not saying much but instead demonstrating mercy (kindness and compassion) to people delivers the message in a far better and cleaner way than talking too much. A whole a lot of hot mess is eliminated when we extend kindness and compassion in lieu of condemnation. Mercy cannot be misunderstood.

Since mercy is one of the attributes of God, when we extend it, people see God in the flesh. People know when they are getting something they don't deserve. When we have mercy on people, we put God in the right light.

Stretch Yourself Out and Show Somebody Uncommon Mercy

It was an ordinary Saturday morning when I realized that I was going to have an assignment of extending mercy on someone. However, it was not the kind of mercy that I had shown to anyone before, especially a total stranger, and I had never shown mercy on a continual basis as I was going to do for this particular woman. On that Saturday, I decided to stop at one of the huge bookstores downtown. I like to read, so I often spend time reading there. This was a same place where I had met an evangelist Mark. My meetings with both of these people were only two weeks apart. Two weeks before I met Mark, I met a woman whom I will call Mary. Mary had more problems than Mark because she was homeless. I forced myself out of my comfort zone and offered to take her home. From what I saw there at the bookstore before I took her home, I realized that she liked to talk and did not like to listen; nevertheless, I went ahead and took her home with me. I let her use the extra room that I reserved for studies and prayer and that, at times, I offered to visitors. This explains how much I felt about my plan being interrupted and my space invaded. After I offered to get her off the street, I quickly learned that she had been in and out of shelters over a long period of time. I was puzzled for a moment but did not change my decision. It took me about a day to realize that, not only was this woman whom I had welcomed into my home rude, but she was also very aggressive and controlling. She lacked social skills and was manipulative and prideful. During the first four weeks of her stay with me, we had had two arguments. The second one left me so exhausted that I was ready to throw her out. Keep in mind that everything that she used in my home was mine except the clothes she wore. Every time she did anything, she said, "God told me"—God told me to make breakfast. God told me to sleep in today. God told me to vacuum. The list of similar comments goes on and on. One day she said, "Oh, I hear the Lord laughing." Some of you are laughing, which is okay. However, this, to me, was not a laughing matter. It was a serious spiritual situation and probably something deeper. Prior to this, I had never met anyone like her.

I soon learned that she had been kicked out of several churches and several homes. I learned that she had been a nightmare to multiple pastors and pastors' wives. Her adult children had banished her from their homes. Moreover, she had been homeless for most of her life. By this time, I wanted her out of my home too. I could not live like that; besides, I had a very good reason. So, I went to God in prayer and asked Him what I should do next. He answered me by impressing this scripture into my heart: "Blessed are the merciful for they shall obtain mercy." That was not what I expected. With my burdened heart, I told God, "I want to, Lord, but I am weary. Help me." She lived in my home for three months. Some days were better than other days. And

70

I was determined that she would continue to be there until the day I felt led that it was okay for me to ask her to leave. God helped me to have mercy on that woman every day. I didn't know how long the situation was going to go on, but one thing I knew was this: I had made up my mind not to quit. This was the first time in my life that I had learned extensively in such a very personal level what it means to have mercy on someone on a daily basis who, in my opinion, was absolutely not worthy of mercy. It became necessary for me to exercise a different sort of lifestyle.

I had welcomed this woman into my home, and obviously into my life, and God did bless me tremendously, and this solidified the truth of the principle of mercy. I had mercy on that woman, and in return I received mercy too. I saw doors open where I did not even know that they existed. I received so many blessings that I knew for sure that they were directly connected to my opening the doors of my home to that troubled stranger. The Bible says, "Do not forget to entertain strangers, for by so *doing* some have unwittingly entertained angels" (Hebrews 13:2). Mary knew certain truths from God's word that, at the time, I didn't know because no one had taught me. When she had good days, she introduced me to certain scriptures and offered a fresh understanding that forever changed my life. I was able to use the little that she shared to study more about the topics from more advanced Bible teachers and grow in my knowledge of the Word of God. There are many blessings that I am enjoying today because I extended mercy to a total stranger.

Was it risky? Yes, it was very risky, as are so are many things in this life. While we exercise caution, we must also make room for the Holy Spirit to work in our lives and in the lives of others. It is always important to take precautions; however, we must always leave a room for faith in God and His ability to protect us. The message I want to impart in your life is that, no matter which way you choose to have mercy on others, the truth of God's Word remains today: have mercy on others and He will have mercy on you!

CHAPTER 10

WHAT SHALL WE DO THEN?

> But the mercy of the Lord is from everlasting
> to everlasting On those who fear Him, And
> His righteousness to children's children, To
> such as keep His covenant, And to those
> who remember His commandments to do
> them. (Psalm 103:17–18)

Should we despise and take for granted the mercy that is available to us? I pray not. The Bible says, "Or do you despise the riches of His goodness, forbearance, and longsuffering, not knowing that the goodness of God leads you to repentance?" (Romans 2:4).

This should be taken as warning that, if we treat the mercy of God with contempt, whether it comes directly from Him or indirectly through other people, then we will face His justice.

SHOW MERCY WHILE YOU CAN

Moreover, at other times we may not be permitted to show mercy on others as it is not always within our power to do so. This means that sometimes we will have the opportunity to give mercy and sometimes we will not. Nevertheless, to truly love our neighbors and others and be able to demonstrate true mercy, we must be willing to make ourselves available so that, to the point we are able, we may demonstrate the same loving-kindness that God has shown us. For the Bible says, "Do not withhold good from those to whom it is due, When it is in the power of your hand to do so. Do not say to your neighbor, 'Go, and come back, And tomorrow I will give it,' When you have it with you" (Proverbs 3:27–28).

In some situations, the judgment has already been passed and put in motion as it was in the case of King David when he numbered Israel. In this case, we may have to suffer some if not all the consequences. In King David's issue, the reason that mercy did not have a place over him was because of his iniquity. There is a big difference between sin and iniquity. Sin is a transgression of the law, but iniquity is what we do whenever we excuse or cover our sin. In short, excusing one's sin is iniquity. David knew what he was doing was wrong. Nevertheless, he went ahead and did it anyway even after he was reminded that it was wrong. Here is the biblical account:

Now Satan stood up against Israel, and moved David to number Israel. So David said to Joab and to the leaders of the people, "Go, number Israel from Beersheba to Dan, and bring the number of them to me that I may know it." And Joab answered, "May the Lord make His people a hundred times more than they are. But, my lord the king, are they not all my lord's servants? Why then does my lord require this thing? Why should he be a cause of guilt in Israel?" Nevertheless the king's word prevailed against Joab. Therefore, Joab departed and went throughout all Israel and came to Jerusalem. Then Joab gave the sum of the number of the people to David. All Israel had one million one hundred thousand men who drew the sword, and Judah had four hundred and seventy thousand men who drew the sword. But he did not count Levi and Benjamin among them, for the king's word was abominable to Joab. And God was displeased with this thing; therefore He struck Israel. So David said to God, "I have sinned greatly, because I have done this thing; but now, I pray, take away the iniquity of Your servant, for I have done very foolishly." Then the Lord spoke to Gad, David's seer, saying, "Go and tell David, saying, 'Thus says the Lord : "I offer you three things; choose one of them for yourself, that I may do it to you. So Gad came to David and said to him, "Thus says the Lord: 'Choose for yourself, either three years of famine, or three months to be defeated by your foes with the sword of your enemies overtaking you, or else for three days the sword of the Lord—the plague in the land, with the angel of the Lord destroying throughout all the territory of Israel.' Now consider what answer I should take back to Him who sent me." And David said to Gad, "I am in great distress. Please let me fall into the hand of the Lord, for His mercies are very great; but do not let me fall into the hand of man." So the Lord sent a plague upon Israel, and seventy thousand men of Israel fell. And God sent an angel to Jerusalem to destroy it. As he was destroying, the Lord looked and relented of the disaster, and said to the angel who was destroying, "It is enough; now restrain your hand." And the angel of the Lord stood by the threshing floor of Ornan the Jebusite. Then David lifted his eyes and saw the angel of the Lord standing between earth and heaven, having in his hand a drawn sword stretched out over Jerusalem. So David and the elders, clothed in sackcloth, fell on their faces. And David said to God, "Was it not I who commanded the people

to be numbered? I am the one who has sinned and done evil indeed; but these sheep, what have they done? Let Your hand, I pray, O Lord my God, be against me and my father's house, but not against Your people that they should be plagued."
(1 Chronicles 21:1–17)

This applies to us too. When we know clearly that something is wrong and we insist on doing it even after we have been reminded that it is wrong, we will suffer the consequences. And this is where mercy will not show up. Iniquity chases away the mercy of God but stirs up the wrath of God. This is why, although King David repented, he still had to pay the price for what he did. In this case, God Himself limited His mercy on David. At other times, He may limit us too, especially if we keep excusing our sin.

DON'T ALLOW YOURSELF TO BE SILENCED

Outside voices can be a hindrance to experiencing God's best, which can come into your life when you ask for mercy. Sometimes, you must cut through the noise of distractions and opposition and project your voice to be heard by the mercy giver, Jesus. Keep in mind that the people who are trying to silence you are not the ones who have to stay up at night because of so much pain. They are not the ones who have to file bankruptcy after practicing bad money habits.

They are not the ones who are about to get divorced because they can't break bad patterns in a relationship. Those people cannot cure you of your problems. Your pastor, rabbi, spouse, boss, children, neighbors, teachers, and bankers can't do it for you. That responsibility of a new day in your life rests in your voice. That is what the two blind men did as we previously read in Mathew 20:29–34:

> Now as they went out of Jericho, a great multitude followed Him. And behold, two blind men sitting by the road, when they heard that Jesus was passing by, cried out, saying, "Have mercy on us, O Lord, Son of David!" Then the multitude warned them that they should be quiet; but they cried out all the more, saying, "Have mercy on us, O Lord, Son of David!" So Jesus stood still and called them, and said, "What do you want Me to do for you?" They said to Him, "Lord, that our eyes may be opened." So Jesus had compassion and touched their eyes. And immediately their eyes received sight, and they followed Him.

Just like these two blind men, you must raise your voice and cry out for mercy. The responsibility is yours. The same God who heard the cry for mercy for the two blind men, He will hear your cry for mercy. God will have compassion on you.

SOMETIMES WE ARE NOT
ABLE TO SHOW MERCY

Keep in mind that, though we may be bound to will mercy to all, we may not be bound to give or show mercy, as God may purposely limit us. Remember: God is the author of mercy, and He gets to decide who is granted and who is denied. "So then it is not of him who wills, nor of him who runs, but of God who shows mercy" (Romans 9:16).

LOOK FOR MERCY AND ASK
FOR IT TO MULTIPLY

As you have come to the end of this book, I want to encourage you to look for mercy for your life, family members, job, business, relationship, career, ministry, children, and any other areas of your life that come to mind. I encourage you to look for mercy, but I also encourage you to ask for mercy to multiply in these areas. As the scripture says, "Keep yourselves in the love of God, looking for the mercy of our Lord Jesus Christ unto eternal life. Mercy, peace, and love be multiplied to you" (Jude 1:21,3).

ABOUT THE AUTHOR

Through her thirteen years of ministry, Caster Mtwale has been an inspiring voice in the body of Christ in encouraging, motivating, teaching, and inspiring people to grow in the knowledge and love of God. Born and raised Catholic, she entered in the personal relationship with Jesus when she was just a teen. It was from the gospel of salvation that she heard from her friend's mother who gave her the invitation to come closer to Jesus and challenged her to genuinely live her life for God. She is a founder of The Word & Prayer Ministries, Inc., which reaches people in the greater Denver area and beyond.

Printed in the United States
by Baker & Taylor Publisher Services